W9-AQV-614

Date: 9/13/11

J 394 .2663 MUR
Murray, Julie,
Christmas /

Christmas

ABDO
Publishing Company

A Buddy Book
by
Julie Murray

Visit us at
www.abdopub.com

Published by Buddy Books, an imprint of ABDO Publishing Company, 4940 Viking Drive, Suite 622, Edina, Minnesota 55435. Copyright © 2003 by Abdo Consulting Group, Inc. International copyrights reserved in all countries. No part of this book may be reproduced in any form without written permission from the publisher.

Printed in the United States.

Edited by: Christy DeVillier
Contributing Editors: Matt Ray, Michael P. Goecke
Graphic Design: Denise Esner
Image Research: Deborah Coldiron
Cover Photograph: Corbis
Interior Photographs: Corbis, Hulton Archives, Image Ideas, North Wind Picture Archives, Photodisc

Library of Congress Cataloging-in-Publication Data

Murray, Julie, 1969-
   Christmas/Julie Murray.
      p. cm. — (Holidays. Set 1)
   Includes bibliographical references and index.
   Contents: What is Christmas? — The history of Christmas — How Christmas came to be — The Christmas story — Santa Claus — Christmas stockings — Christmas trees — Other traditions — Christmas around the world.
   ISBN 1-57765-951-1
      1. Christmas—Juvenile literature. [1. Christmas. 2. Holidays.] I. Title.

GT4985.5 .M77 2003
394.2663—dc21

2002027752

Table of Contents

What Is Christmas?

People around the world celebrate Christmas. It is a joyful **holiday**. It is a time for gathering with family and friends. It is a time for sharing with others. People celebrate Christmas with gifts, decorations, parties, carols, and sweets.

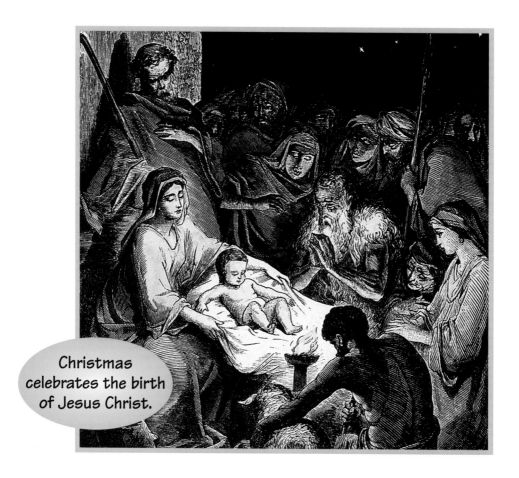

Christmas celebrates the birth of Jesus Christ.

Christmas is a **Christian holiday**. It celebrates the birth of Jesus Christ. Many people believe Jesus was born about 2,000 years ago. But no one is sure of his true birthday. Many people celebrate Christmas on December 25th.

The Christmas Story

There is a **Bible** story about the birth of Jesus Christ. In this story, an angel visited a young woman. The young woman's name was Mary. The angel told Mary that she would have a baby. The angel said that Mary's baby would be the Son of God.

Jesus was born in a stable.

Mary's husband was Joseph. They lived in a town called Nazareth. They had to go to Bethlehem for a **census**. In Bethlehem, Mary and Joseph could not find a place to spend the night. But an innkeeper let them stay in his stable, or barn. That night, Jesus was born.

On the same night, an angel appeared to some shepherds. The angel told them about Jesus. They hurried to go see the Son of God.

Three kings visited Jesus, too. They are also called the "three wise men." They followed a bright star in the sky to find Jesus. They brought gold and other gifts.

A bright star led the three wise men to baby Jesus.

How Christmas Began

Festivals in December were common thousands of years ago. Many December festivals celebrated the end of the **harvest**.

Long ago, the Romans celebrated Saturnalia. Saturnalia began on December 17th. It lasted through the winter solstice. The winter solstice is the shortest day of the year.

Many people decorate their homes for Christmas.

Saturnalia honored the Roman god Saturn. Saturn was the god of farming. The Romans decorated their homes with green branches. They made special meals and traded gifts. Singing and dancing were also common.

Over the years, the **Christian** religion grew. Christians did not pray to the Roman and Greek gods. They did not want to celebrate Saturnalia and other non-Christian festivals. So, they created their own December **holiday**, Christmas.

By the year 1100, Christmas was an important holiday in Europe. Christians held a religious service on December 25th. They called it *Cristes Maesse*. It means "Mass of Christ" or "Christ's Mass." This is where the name Christmas comes from.

Singing hymns is common at Christmas mass.

Saint Nicholas

Saint Nicholas lived about 1,600 years ago. He was a leader in the **Christian** church. Many people believe Nicholas helped children. He may have given gifts to the poor. The **legend** of Saint Nicholas's good deeds became famous.

After he died, **Christians** called Nicholas a **saint**. Many celebrated his kindness on December 6th. Over time, Saint Nicholas stood for giving during Christmas. Christmas "good will" and helping others may have started with Saint Nicholas.

Saint Nicholas is famous for his good deeds.

Many Europeans still celebrate **Saint** Nicholas's Day today. People in the Netherlands call Saint Nicholas Sinter Klaas. Parents tell their children stories about Sinter Klaas. They say he visits homes on December 5th. Dutch children believe Sinter Klaas leaves gifts for them.

Dutch settlers brought their **customs** to the United States years ago. Americans began celebrating Sinter Klaas, too. Over time, American children began calling Sinter Klaas Santa Claus.

Christmas Stockings

Some children hang Christmas stockings on Christmas Eve. A story about **Saint** Nicholas explains this **custom**. He wanted to secretly help poor families. So, he threw gold coins down their chimneys. The coins fell into their stockings hanging by the fire. Today, children hope Saint Nicholas will fill their stockings with gifts.

Christmas Trees

Today, many people decorate evergreen trees for Christmas. This **custom** may have started in Germany about 400 years ago. The Germans decorated their Christmas trees with lit candles. They brought this custom to the United States.

Decorating trees for Christmas is an old custom.

Scotch pines, firs, and spruces are common Christmas trees. Today, people decorate Christmas trees with electric lights. Candy canes, bows, and strings of popcorn are common decorations, too. Store-bought or homemade, Christmas tree decorations can be almost anything.

Christmas Today

People around the world celebrate Christmas in many ways. In Sweden, the Christmas season begins on December 13th with **Saint** Lucia's Day. Saint Lucia is the saint of light. On this morning, girls and boys wear white clothes. The oldest daughter wears a crown of lit candles. Then she serves breakfast to everyone.

Singing Christmas carols is common in many countries.

In Australia, some people celebrate Christmas with a picnic on the beach. There are Christmas fireworks in the Philippines and Guatemala. In Greece, children go from house to house singing.

Christmas **customs** may change from country to country. But Christmas is a joyful **holiday** wherever it is celebrated.

Important Words

Bible a holy book of the Christian religion.

census the task of counting people of a country and gathering facts about them.

Christian describes anything tied to Christianity, a religion that follows the teachings of Jesus Christ.

custom a practice that has been around a long time. Decorating a tree is one custom of Christmas.

harvest a time for gathering crops.

holiday a special time of celebration.

legend an old story that cannot be proven to be true.

saint a holy person.

Web Sites

To learn more about Christmas,
visit ABDO Publishing Company on the World Wide Web. Web site links about Christmas are featured on our Book Links page. These links are routinely monitored and updated to provide the most current information available.

www.abdopub.com

Index